How To Write
Your Autobiography

How To Write Your Autobiography

Preserving Your Family Heritage

By Patricia Ann Case

Published by
Woodbridge Press Publishing Company
Santa Barbara, California 93111

1995

Published and distributed by

Woodbridge Press Publishing Company
Post Office Box 209
Santa Barbara, California 93102

Copyright © 1977 by Patricia Ann Case

Library of Congress Catalog Card Number: 77-72670

International Standard Book Number: 0-912800-38-0

Distributed simultaneously in the United States and Canada.

Printed in the United States of America.

My Thanks

The pages of this book are the result of many seemingly isolated events—a boy missing his grandparents, the anecdotes of a skating costume designer, unexpected visits from friends, a set of books received as a birthday present, a family whose jobs drew them miles apart. In its own way, each of these events pointed out to me the need for a family to preserve its own heritage.

It is impossible to name everyone involved in making this book a reality, but the following people deserve individual thanks and credit, even though when we talked neither they nor I realized they were contributing to the formation of the idea for this guide. First, my son, without whom the need for preserving our heritage would not have become apparent; second, my encouraging and supportive husband; third, my enthusiastic friends who asked how they could get their parents to write their life stories; next, my entire family—especially my always-loving mother and three sisters—who underscored the value of Grandma's story; and last but very importantly, Nora Bell Smith, the great-grandmother who at age seventy-five unassumingly wrote about her life—for the family for whom she has lived her life.

Contents

Preface

Autobiography and Self-Identity

Tracing one's family history and genealogy is not only one of the largest hobbies in the United States, it is rapidly developing into an important technique in today's social science fields. In anthropology, for example, tracing and recording family histories is useful in discovering what elements contribute to the social mobility of immigrant and minority families.

Recent studies using the family history "technique" have shown that children of those families who maintain contact with broad kinship bases achieve greater social mobility than children who lose family kinship ties.

In education, discovering one's family background helps students to establish a sense of personal identity and self-worth. Courses in developing one's family background are being offered in social studies departments of some secondary schools. In more limited respects, the idea is used even in life science classrooms to help students establish their genetic inheritances. In the future I would like to see the technique extended to help young juvenile delinquents gain a sense of personal worth and dignity.

Some psychologists, believing that no individual is an island in the realm of analysis, now ask entire families to join in treatment. Family psycho-history is a growing sub-field of psychological therapy.

The autobiographies of parents and grandparents can be valuable in providing information to the family's children for any number of reasons—from merely the delight of a hobby to aiding in medical treatment. Eminent authorities such as Dr. Margaret Mead, Mrs. Scottie Fitzgerald Smith, Dr. Mary Matossian, Dr. Jean Gilbert and Dr. G. Wesley Johnson have recognized the importance of preserving a family's background and personal history.

Individual autobiographies provide insights that contribute to the family both now and as they are passed along to following generations. An autobiography provides a unique outlook that helps to establish a family identity, a foundation that can influence the members of that family for ages to come.

Part I

Preserving Your Personal History

Chapter 1

The Need for Writing Your Life Story

Among the most valuable gifts you can give
your children and grandchildren are the stories
of your life. When families lived together or
close together, this gift was given by word of
mouth—the grandchildren were near and
frequently asking to be told a story. Night after
night during the years I lived with her, my
grandmother told me stories of her childhood.
Then, too, as I tagged along behind her
in the daytime I learned her ways of doing
things and coping with problems. When she
took me on special outings, I learned the value
of her entertainments. I tagged along after
Grandpa, too—for the fun of it, I thought then.

As I realized later, however, I was picking up ways of doing things which eventually became guidelines of comparison for me.

Parents, of course, show ways of doing things and give comparison guidelines to children too, but they do it differently than grandparents. First, there often is a more authoritative tone to the instructions of parents, who are directly responsible for the children. For grandparents, on the other hand, association with the grandchildren is usually voluntary. Grandparents do not shoulder full responsibility for the grandchildren, so they can be more carefree and relaxed.

Second, parents must deal with all the details of busy, day-to-day life for their children. Grandparents, in contrast, have had more years and often more leisure to sift through and come up with those ideas that, in hindsight, have proven most important.

Third, of necessity, most parents are involved with the modern methods of living: of heating the home, keeping and preparing food, transportation. Without grandparents' stories of the "good ol'days" showing that there were other ways of accomplishing daily living chores, children become fixed in the present methods. If Grandpa, however, had a spring house to keep the milk cool, then the grandchildren know that a spring house, as well as a refrigerator, can preserve food because, well, Grandpa did it that way. Grandchildren learn that a wood stove can heat a house, that people used to travel by foot, horse and wagon, or street car, because Grandpa and Grandma did, and here they are telling about it.

During the past two generations this country has progressed rapidly from a rural to an urban society. With energy and food crises becoming more evident, children are seeing that such "progress" cannot long continue. Many are beginning to question modern ways of living. They are saying, "Hey, what was done before we had supermarkets? How was food preserved and distributed? How did people survive cold winters before natural gas and oil, before central heating?" It is valuable for each family's ways to be recorded.

Also because of the rapid urbanization of our country, many families are separated. Grandparents are too often names, occasional visits, letters, voices at the other end of a long distance phone call. But there is a way you can give your experiences to your grand-children—you can write them down, even if you think you can't write.

Here is what happened in my family. Sad that my son was missing out on the wonderful stories I had heard as a child, I asked my grandmother to write down the stories she had told me so that I could read them to my son. Grandma protested that she had no training as a writer, and finished only eight grades, and wouldn't know how to put the stories on paper. The result was that we worked out a plan. If I would help her organize them, she would write the stories. Since she lived hundreds of miles away, this presented a problem. After several months, I developed an idea and mailed my suggestion to Grandma. It seemed to provide just the organization she needed. She went right to work, writing a couple of hours a day when she felt good. When we went to visit her at Easter, she read to me and my sisters the draft of what she had written. The whole family was enthusiastic about Grandma's stories and we were anxious for her to continue.

One summer day, a box arrived in the mail. It was Grandma's autobiography, all finished. She had mailed it to me first, with the request that I mail it to each of my sisters and cousins after reading it (we are quite a large, scattered family). Well, my son and I wanted to read it over and over so we thought, why not publish several copies so every member could have his own book? That became our project. We made copies, fastened them together, added prints we had made of the treasured pictures, and then bound the copies in hard covers. Those books were the most cherished Christmas presents received by anyone in the entire family that year.

The responses of our family to our grandmother's autobiography showed me what treasures each grandparent holds, and made me begin thinking that perhaps with some help, every person—especially a grandparent—could share his or her unique stories with their family. Even if someone else has already prepared the family's genealogy, your own experiences and viewpoints are invaluable and should be written.

As stated before, writing an autobiography has value for passing along ways of doing things, but it also is worthwhile in another, perhaps more important way. That is, it increases one's sense of identity—especially so of grandchildren as time goes on. They get to know their grandparents' backgrounds and ideas, which gives them better insight into their own beginnings and thus into themselves. It also can give your children and grandchildren a sense of family continuity and solidity even through frequent moving or across thousands of of miles.

Chapter 2

How To Write Your Autobiography

With the foregoing values in mind, I've adapted the guide I gave my grandmother to get her started writing, and have composed an outline to help you, your parents, or your grandparents to write the stories of your life and "publish" them yourself.

To give the unique gift of your own story to your children and grandchildren, go over the following instructions carefully. Read them several times before proceeding. Then read over the guide questions in each chapter several times and think about how you will answer them. Now you are ready to write. Remember, you are creating a gift that no one else can ever give to your family.

Practical Suggestions

Here are some practical suggestions to help you write your story clearly and naturally:

1. Use pen or soft (#2) pencil, whichever is more comfortable for you to use. Don't worry about typing—your children and grandchildren will value your own handwriting far more.

2. Answer the questions asked on the guide pages. Start with the first question and work through to the last question. Take your time, work only while you feel fresh and alert. If you tire, stop and take a break until you feel like writing again.

3. Number each page *before* you start writing on it. That way you won't forget and then later get the pages mixed up.

4. Put in dates, places. These are your family's history. If you don't write them down, your grandchildren may never know when or where an event took place.

5. Put in details—colors, sizes, kinds of materials, textures. Describe things and places with so much detail that your children or grandchildren can almost "see them before their eyes."

6. Write how you felt. When you describe events that happened, don't just tell the events, also describe your feelings while it was happening, and how you felt afterward.

7. Though feelings are important it is wise to remember that what you are writing will be read to and handed down to future generations. You don't want to perpetuate any family feuds or to hurt anyone's feelings.

8. Though you don't want to write harshly about other people, do be honest about your living conditions. If times were hard, tell about them and how you coped with them. Remember that your purpose is not to write a dreamy picture of a perfect life, but to write about your problems and good times so that you help give your children or grandchildren a basis for comparison and decision-making.

9. In addition to actions and feelings, write your thoughts about life. If your experiences have shown that certain ways are right and certain others are wrong, write down your conclusions and your reasons for them. After all, because you've lived as long as you have, you must have developed some guidelines and philosophies of living.

10. When you tell about a former way of doing something, list the steps it took to do it and describe the equipment you used in detail. For example:

"To make snow ice cream here's what we did when we awoke to a new-fallen snow:

"a. We hurriedly put on our dresses, stockings, shoes, sweaters, and wool scarves. (Since we would be out only a few minutes we didn't need leggings, coats, or mittens.)

"b. Then we'd run into the big warm kitchen where Grandma was cooking breakfast and all three of us at once would ask her if we could make snow ice cream.

"c. She would give each of us an eight-inch tin pie pan and a big spoon and then tell us to find a patch of clean snow in the backyard where no one had walked, no ashes or twigs had fallen, and then to gently scrape just the top layer of snow with the spoon, being careful not to scoop down to the dried grass or dirt.

"d. When we went outside, we tiptoed around the snow until we found just the right patch, usually under the bare branches of the cherry tree. Next, being careful not to step in the middle of our patch, we each carefully spooned new clean snow into our pans, while Grandma watched from the kitchen window.

"e. After our pans were filled we went up the steep back porch stairs and handed our pans to Grandma. As we took off our scarves and got warm by the high-legged pink porcelain gas cooking stove, Grandma would sprinkle sugar over each pan of snow and add a few drops of vanilla extract.

"f. Then came the best part of all—eating our delicious snow ice cream before it melted. When the last cold bite had trickled down our throats we were ready for our breakfast of big bowls of warm oatmeal, hot fried eggs, toast, and home-canned peaches."

The idea is to put in all the details so that, if it were possible, your own children or grandchildren could go out in a new-fallen snow and make snow ice cream (or whatever) exactly as you did it.

11. Write like you talk. Remember, you're telling your story to your family—make it sound like you're talking to them. Don't try to make it stiff and formal like an essay. Put in your favorite sayings. My grandpa always said, "Well, I declare!" whenever we would run up to him and tell him a wonderful new discovery.

12. If you write like you talk, you'll automatically take care of sentences and punctuation. Wherever you would pause in talking, put a comma in your writing. When you finish a thought, put a period. When you start a new thought, begin with a capital letter. If you're writing about what you or someone else said, put a comma after the word said, and quotation marks before the first word they said and after the last word they said. For example, Cousin Mary said, "My word, there's a skunk on the front step!"

That's about all there is to ordinary punctuation except to use a question mark instead of a period when you ask a question or to put an exclamation point at the end of a sentence that expresses strong feelings. If you want to get fancy with colons and semi-colons, get a writer's handbook such as *The Practical Stylist,* by Sheridan Baker, or *A Manual of Style* published by The University of Chicago Press.

13. Many people fret over writing paragraphs. That shouldn't bother you. Each anecdote or event that you write about can be a complete paragraph. If you're writing about a very long event you can make the beginning, middle, and end each a separate paragraph. For example:

"In second grade the school day seemed to drag and drag. The bell rang at 8:30 and we all

lined up in the cold outside the side door. Then
we would march through the basement hall, up
the stairs, along the first floor hall, and into
Room Five's cloakroom. There we would
struggle to get our galoshes, leggings, coats,
sweaters, and wet mittens off. Then we'd slip
into our desks in Room Five, say good morning
to Miss Weldon, stand, salute the flag, and sing
"America, the Beautiful." By this time it was
only 8:45. Next, we opened our little side
drawers, and took out our tablets and our big
fat black pencils to copy arithmetic problems
from the blackboard. Then we'd put away our
arithmetic and do spelling with our big fat black
pencils. Finally, it would be recess time but in
bad weather that only meant getting out the
boxes of checkers for fifteen minutes, and then
back to work on handwriting with our big fat
black pencils. By this time we knew it was only
11:00 because our stomachs would start
growling and the first delicious smells would
start drifting up from the basement cafeteria.
Somehow the hour dragged on.

"Lunchtime at last! Boys and girls made
separate lines and went to their respective rest
rooms and wash areas. Then those buying went
to the cafeteria line while those who brought
went back upstairs to the room and ate at their
desks with Miss Weldon. Next, it was
playtime—in the gym during wet weather. All
too soon, it seemed, playtime was over.

"Then we trudged back up the stairs to Room Five and slipped into our desks again. Now it was time for reading, then social studies, a short recess, either singing or drawing, and finally, 3:00 would come. Suddenly we would be full of energy and could hardly be quiet enough for Miss Weldon to dismiss us, table by table, quietest ones first. At last the school day was over."

Another way to think about paragraphs is to remember that when you finish writing about one subject, start a new paragraph when you start another subject.

To help out with paragraphing, there is a mark like this ¶ that I have used to show you when it would be logical to start a new paragraph. When you see this mark—¶—before a question in the guide, start a new line and indent the first word about one-half inch. Paragraphs are just logical divisions of your thoughts and aren't so important. The important thing is for you to write your story.

14. Use many transitions. Transitions are words that guide your children or grandchildren through your stories without losing the way.

Here is a list of words and phrases to use:

when	afterwards	since
whenever	again	yet
first	also	indeed
second	too	in fact

third	in addition to	still
fourth	further	that is
last	furthermore	after all
now	moreover	on the other hand
then	likewise	notwithstanding
until	similarly	consequently
next	for example	incidentally
immediately	for instance	hence
previously	though	thus
the preceding	however	therefore
the following	but	in summary

Now you are ready to use the guide outlines in Part II and start writing your story.

Part II

Guides For Writing Your Autobiography

Guides for Writing Your Autobiography

The following guide outlines will help you to recall important details of your life story and to write them in a clear, logical order. Here is how to use the guide outlines:

a. There is an outline page or pages for each chapter of your autobiography. The outline page has questions on it. To start writing you simply take a piece of writing paper and put the page number in the middle of the bottom space. Now you are ready to start writing the answer to the first question in Chapter I of your guide outlines. As you proceed, try to use sheets of paper that are uniform in size, weight, color, etc., so your finished work can be bound up as an attractive "book."

b. Remember when answering each question to include details, thoughts, and feelings.

c. Since you are numbering the pages, there is no limit to the length of the answer you can write. You can make it as long or as brief as you want.

d. Don't worry about wording, fancy handwriting, or spelling—the important thing is to get your autobiography on paper. Later, if you want to change wording or spelling you can rewrite a page. But first get your stories written.

e. Similarly, if you can't remember a name, date, place, or event, leave some space for it and go on writing. Later, when you recall the information you can go back and fill in the space you left.

f. *After* you have answered a question, *check off* the box for that question on the guide outline. That way you can always tell by a quick glance at your guide where to begin writing again.

g. If a certain outline question doesn't apply to your autobiography, simply mark the box and proceed to the next question. If you decide to skip more than one outline question, be sure to check off all the boxes so that you can keep your place.

h. When you have finished checking off the last box of the last chapter, follow the instructions of the outline to compose the appendices. You can have your book bound, if you wish. Then you will have a unique gift to give to your family—a gift that they will cherish forever, a gift that will enrich their lives, but most of all, a gift that *they will never have unless you give it to them.*

Your Autobiography

Chapter 1

Early Childhood

¶1. When were you born? ☐

2. In what town, state, territory, or country were you born? ☐

3. Were there any unusual circumstances about your birth? ☐

4. Were you born in a house, log cabin, dugout, covered wagon, hospital, or taxi cab? ☐

¶5. Who was your mother? ☐

6. Who were her parents? ☐

7. What do you remember about her family? ☐

8. Who were her brothers and sisters? ☐

9. If you can, describe how your mother's parents, brothers, and sisters looked. ☐

10. What kind of people were your mother's family? ☐

11. What special family customs, skills, talents, or traditions did they have? ☐

12. Where was your mother born? ☐

13. When was she born? ☐

14. Where did your mother grow up? ☐

15. What did she like to play or do most when she was a girl? ☐

16. Where did she go to school? ☐

17. How long did she get to attend school? ☐

18. What kinds of jobs did she have? ☐

¶19. Who was your father? ☐

20. Who were his parents? ☐

21. What do you remember about his family? □

22. Who were his brothers and sisters? □

23. If you can, describe how your father's parents, brothers, and sisters looked. □

24. What kind of people were your father's family? □

25. What special family customs, skills, talents, or traditions did they have? □

26. Where was your father born? □

27. When was he born? □

28. Where did your father grow up? □

29. Where did he go to school? □

30. What did he like to play or do most when he was a boy? □

31. How long did he get to attend school? □

32. What kinds of jobs did he have?

¶33. How did your parents meet? □

34. When did they marry? □

35. Where did they live when first married? ☐

36. What kind of work did your father do to support his bride? ☐

37. Did your mother work when first married? ☐

¶38. How many brothers do you have? ☐

39. How many sisters do you have? ☐

40. Who are your brothers and sisters? ☐

41. In what order were you and your brothers and sisters born? ☐

42. What is the birth date of each of your brothers and sisters? ☐

¶43. What is the first thing you can remember? ☐

44. What kinds of toys did you have? ☐

45. What were your favorite toys? ☐

46. What were your favorite nursery rhymes and bedtime stories? ☐

47. What events and playmates do you remember from your preschool days? ☐

48. What was your favorite food when you were little? ☐

49. When did you first start doing chores around home? ☐

50. What kinds of chores did you first have to do? ☐

¶51 What is the first holiday you can remember? ☐

52. What holidays were celebrated by your family? ☐

53. How was each holiday celebrated? ☐

¶54. What do you remember about the house you lived in as a young child? ☐

55. Where was the house located? ☐

56. How long did your family live there? ☐

57. Did you move during your preschool days? If so, how many times? ☐

58. What do you remember about each new home you lived in during your preschool days? ☐

Chapter 2

School Days

¶1. What are the first thoughts you can remember about going to school? ☐

¶2. When did you start school? ☐

3. What school did you go to? ☐

4. Was it a private, parochial, or public school? ☐

5. Did you attend kindergarten or go directly into first grade or your first primer? ☐

¶6. Do you remember what you wore on your first day of school? ☐

7. What were your feelings on your first day of school? □

8. How did you get to school? □

9. How far was it? □

¶10. How big was the school? □

11. How many rooms did your school have? □

12. About how many students were in your school? □

13. Were there separate schools for elementary grades, junior high, and high school, or were all the grades in one school? □

¶14. Describe your first classroom. □

¶16. What were your initial impressions of your first teacher? □

17. What was her name? □

18. After you got to know her (or him), what did you think of your first teacher? □

¶19. Describe what you did during a typical school day. □

20. Did you use chalk and slate, or pencil and paper?   ☐

21. What kinds of books did you use in school?   ☐

¶22. Who were your best friends during your early school years?   ☐

¶23. What were your favorite subjects in school?   ☐

24. What did you do during recess?   ☐

25. What kind of schoolyard was there?   ☐

¶26. What did you have for lunch?   ☐

27. Did you carry your lunch to school?   ☐

¶28. What did you do during summer vacations?   ☐

29. How long did you go to that first school?   ☐

30. Did you move around from school to school or stay in one school for several years?   ☐

¶31. What are the most fun times you remember from your early school years?   ☐

¶32. What are the most disappointing times you remember from your early school years?   ☐

(*Remember to tell events as they were. One of your purposes is to give your children and grandchildren a realistic picture of your life so that they can better understand their own lives.*)

¶33. Did you attend junior high school?   ☐

34. Describe where the junior high was and how it looked.   ☐

35. What were your favorite junior high courses?   ☐

36. What classes did you dislike most in junior high?   ☐

¶37. Do you have any special memories (good or bad) about particular junior high teachers?   ☐

¶38. How many years did you attend junior high school?   ☐

39. If you quit early, what were your main reasons for quitting?   ☐

¶40. Did you work while you attended junior high school?   ☐

41. At what jobs did you work?   ☐

42. How many hours did you work?   ☐

43. What did you get paid for working?   ☐

44. What did you usually do with your pay?   ☐

¶45. What were your favorite pastimes and foods during your elementary and junior high school years?   ☐

46. What were the clothing styles when you were in elementary and junior high school?   ☐

Chapter 3

Teen Years

¶1. Did your family celebrate birthdays? ☐

2. How did they celebrate birthdays? ☐

3. Was there any special celebration for any of your teenage birthdays? ☐

¶4. How did you feel about becoming a teenager? ☐

¶5. What was expected of you as a teenager? ☐

¶6. Did you attend high school? ☐

7. If so, what high school did you attend? ☐

8. Describe how that high school appeared to you. ☐

9. Where was your high school?   ☐

10. How did you get there?   ☐

11. How long did it take you to get to school?   ☐

12. About how big was your high school?   ☐

13. About how many students attended it?   ☐

¶14. How long was each school term?   ☐

15. How long was the school day?   ☐

¶16. Did you have the opportunity to choose any of your courses?   ☐

17. What were your favorite studies, and why?   ☐

18. What were your most disliked studies, and why?   ☐

¶19. What teachers most influenced your thinking, and why?   ☐

20. Who were your favorite high school teachers? Why were they your favorites?   ☐

21. Did you strongly dislike any of your high school teachers? If so, why?   ☐

¶22. Did you have a job while you attended high school? ☐

23. How many hours did you work after school? ☐

24. What kind of work did you do? ☐

25. How much pay did you get? ☐

26. What did you usually do with your pay? ☐

¶27. What did you do during summer vacations from school? ☐

28. What chores were you expected to do at home during the school year? ☐

29. What chores were you expected to do at home during school vacations? ☐

¶30. How long did you attend high school? ☐

31. If you quit before finishing, why did you quit high school? ☐

¶32. Who were your best friends during your teenage years? ☐

¶33. What were the most fun times you had in high school or your teen years? ☐

34. What were the most unpleasant times you
    had in high school or your teen years?   ☐

35. How do your teen years compare with
    present teenagers' lives?   ☐

¶36. What did you do after you no longer
    attended school?   ☐

¶37. Did you attend college?   ☐

*If you attended college, answer questions 38a
through 38ff. If you didn't attend college,
skip to Chapter IV.*

38a.   Why did you decide to attend college?   ☐

¶38b.   What college did you attend?   ☐

38c.   Why did you choose that particular
       college to attend?   ☐

38d.   Where was your college?   ☐

38e.   How many students did it have when you
       attended?   ☐

¶38f.   What were the approximate costs to
       attend your college?   ☐

38g.   How did you meet those costs?   ☐

38h.   Did you have a job while you attended college?   ☐

38i.   What was your job?   ☐

38j.   How much pay did you get per hour?   ☐

38k.   What did you usually do with your pay?   ☐

¶38l.   What was your major in college?   ☐

38m.   Why did you choose that major?   ☐

38n.   If you had a minor, what was it?   ☐

¶38o.   What were your favorite college courses?   ☐

¶38p.   Who were your favorite professors, and why?   ☐

38q.   Do you feel that one particular professor influenced your decisions or life? How and why?   ☐

¶38r.   Where did you live while you attended college?   ☐

¶38s.   How many years did you attend college?   ☐

38t.   If you quit college, why did you quit?   ☐

38u.   If you graduated, when did you graduate?   ☐

38v.   What special memories do you have of your college graduation?   ☐

¶38w. What are your favorite memories of college?   ☐

¶38x. Did you attend graduate school?   ☐

38y.   If so, what was your graduate specialty?   ☐

38z.   Where did you attend graduate school?   ☐

38aa. How long did you attend graduate school?   ☐

38bb. What advanced degrees, if any, did you earn?   ☐

¶38cc. How did you live while in graduate school?   ☐

38dd. How did you pay your expenses while you were in graduate school?   ☐

¶38ee. What are your thoughts about the value of college in a person's life?   ☐

38ff. What advice would you give your children or grandchildren regarding college?   ☐

Chapter 4

Becoming a Young Adult

¶1. By the time you were a young adult, what changes had taken place in the ways of life since the time you were little?   ☐

  2. Were there any major changes in your family's way of living?   ☐

  3. What modern conveniences, if any, had your family acquired by this time?   ☐

¶4. Were there any apparent trends such as people moving to cities or away from the cities?   ☐

¶5. What was happening nationally at this time?   ☐

¶6. What was happening internationally at this time?   ☐

7. Were there any wars? If so, what wars were there?   ☐

8. Did you or any of your family have to go to war?   ☐

9. If so, how long were you or your family member away at war?   ☐

10. Where were you or your family member stationed during the war?   ☐

11. What happened to you or your family member during the war?   ☐

¶12. After you finished your schooling, what was your first job?   ☐

13. Was it a full or part-time job?   ☐

14. How did you get your job?   ☐

15. Where was your job?   ☐

16. How did you get to work and home again?   ☐

17. How long was your working day?   ☐

¶18. If you weren't working away from home, what were your duties at home? ☐

19. How long did you live at home? ☐

20. When did you leave home? ☐

21. How did you feel when you were out on your own? ☐

¶22. As a young adult, what plans or dreams did you have for your future? ☐

23. Why did you think of those plans or dreams for your future? ☐

24. Did you think you would be able to accomplish them? ☐

25. What did you do, if anything, toward accomplishing your plans or dreams while you were a young adult? ☐

¶26. Looking back, what do you think was most important to you at this point in your young adult life? ☐

¶27. How old were you when you first became aware of the opposite sex? ☐

28. What kinds of courting customs were there when you were dating? ☐

29. Who was your first sweetheart?   ☐

30. Where was your first sweetheart from?   ☐

¶31. When did you meet your future spouse?   ☐

32. Where did you meet your future spouse?   ☐

33. Where did you go when you were courting?   ☐

34. When did you begin to realize that you were in love?   ☐

35. How did you become engaged?   ☐

36. When did you become engaged?   ☐

37. How did your family feel about your engagement?   ☐

38. How did your future spouse's family feel about your engagement?   ☐

39. How long were you engaged?   ☐

¶40. What were the reasons for setting the particular date for your wedding?   ☐

41. Did you decide that you had to have so much savings, or a certain amount of land, or a job before you would marry?   ☐

¶42. How did you plan your wedding?   ☐

43. Who helped most in planning your wedding?   ☐

44. Were there any pre-wedding showers or parties?   ☐

¶45. When was your wedding?   ☐

46. Where were you married?   ☐

47. Who performed the ceremony?   ☐

48. What kind of ceremony was it?   ☐

49. Who were the bride's and groom's attendants?   ☐

¶50. Describe your wedding clothes.   ☐

51. Describe your spouse's wedding clothes.   ☐

52. How did you feel during the ceremony?   ☐

53. Is there any particular part of the ceremony that you especially remember?   ☐

¶54. How many guests attended the ceremony?   ☐

55. Who were the guests you remember?   ☐

56. Was there a reception or party after the ceremony?   ☐

57. What do you especially remember about the reception or party? ☐

¶58. Where did you spend your honeymoon? ☐

59. What do you especially remember about your honeymoon? ☐

¶60. Where did you live when you were first married? ☐

61. Was it a house or an apartment? ☐

62. What kind of furniture did you have? ☐

63. How did you obtain your household linens and dishes? ☐

¶64. Did you have a budget to live on? ☐

65. Do you remember what your budget was and how you managed on it? ☐

66. What was the most difficult part of managing the household expenses? ☐

¶67. What do you remember as being the most difficult part of adjusting to married life? ☐

68. What were your biggest marital quarrels about? ☐

69. How did you resolve marital arguments? ☐

70. Do you have a formula for working out marital problems? ☐

¶71. In the early years of your marriage, what qualities did you most admire in your spouse? ☐

72. What do you feel helped you most during the early years of your marriage? ☐

¶73. Were there any serious illnesses or economic hardships during your early married life? If so, describe them. ☐

¶74. What special memories or stories do you have of the early days of your marriage? ☐

Chapter 5

Starting a Family

¶1. What were your plans or dreams for raising a family? ☐

2. How many children did you want to have? ☐

3. How many girls did you want? ☐

4. How many boys did you want? ☐

5. What methods of family planning or child-spacing were available to you? ☐

6. What kind of preparation did you have for being a parent?   ☐

7. What were your ideas about the kind of parent you wanted to be to your children?   ☐

¶8. When did you suspect that your first child was on the way?   ☐

9. How did you tell your spouse (or how did your spouse tell you) about the pregnancy?   ☐

10. How was the news received by your family and your spouse's family?   ☐

¶11. Did you (your wife) go to a doctor right away?   ☐

12. Were there any pregnancy complications?   ☐

13. If so, how were they treated?   ☐

14. What kind of pre-natal medical treatment was there in those days?   ☐

¶15. How did you get ready for the baby's arrival?   ☐

16. Where did you get baby clothes?   ☐

17. What kind of baby clothes and diapers did you have for your baby?   ☐

18. Did you (your wife) have to give up a job because of the pregnancy? ☐

19. If so, what did this do to your budget or living standard? ☐

¶20. Where was your first baby born? ☐

21. What preparations were necessary for the birth? ☐

22. If the birth was at home, what preparations were made? ☐

23. Who helped out with the birth? ☐

24. Did a doctor or midwife attend the delivery? Who was he or she? ☐

25. Were there any complications during the birth? If so, what? ☐

26. What was the total cost of the birth? ☐

¶27. When was the baby born? ☐

28. Was it a girl or a boy? ☐

29. What did you name her or him? ☐

30. How did you pick out the name? ☐

31. What were your feelings when you first saw your baby? ☐

¶32. How long was your (your wife's) convalescence after the birth? ☐

34. What changes did the birth of the baby bring into the household? ☐

35. How long did it take for your new family to settle into a comfortable routine? ☐

¶36. What were the first noticeable personality traits of your new baby? ☐

37. How would you describe the baby's behavior and health? ☐

¶38. When did the responsibilities of being a parent become realities for you? ☐

39. What did you most enjoy about being a new parent? ☐

40. What are some of the stories you remember about your early experiences as a parent? ☐

¶41. When did your second child arrive? ☐

42. How was the arrival of your second child different from that of your firstborn? ☐

43. Were there any birth complications? ☐

44. What did you name your second child? ☐

45. Why did you choose that name? ☐

¶46. What were your feelings about the birth of your second child? ☐

47. How did your first child react to the arrival of your second child? ☐

48. What special stories do you remember about your second child? ☐

¶49. Were there any more children in your family? ☐

50. When was each child born? ☐

51. What name did you give to each child and why did you choose that name? ☐

¶52. What special stories do you remember about each child? ☐

Chapter 6

Raising a Family

¶1. Did you have to move to a larger house or apartment as your family grew? ☐

2. Did you (or your spouse) have to change jobs or get extra work to provide for your family? ☐

3. How did you and your spouse manage to feed and clothe your children as they were growing up? ☐

¶4. What were your children's favorite meals? ☐

5. What were your children's favorite games or pastimes?   ☐

6. What styles of clothing did your daughter (s) wear?   ☐

7. What styles of clothing did your son (s) wear?   ☐

8. What kinds of chores did your children have to do?   ☐

¶9. What childhood illnesses did the children have?   ☐

10. How did you cope with the illnesses? (*Give details so your children or grandchildren can compare with treatment available today.*)   ☐

¶11. Where did your children attend school?   ☐

12. Compare the changes that had taken place from the time when you went to school to when your children attended school.   ☐

¶13. What kinds of vacations did your family have?   ☐

14. What kinds of holiday celebrations did your family have?   ☐

15. Which holidays did the children like most? ☐

16. Which holidays did you enjoy most? ☐

¶17. What did you think was important for your children to learn as they were growing up? ☐

18. How did you discipline your children? ☐

19. What kinds of worries did you have as a parent? ☐

¶20. What do you think was the most difficult part of raising your family? ☐

¶21. What did you want for yourself while your children were growing up? ☐

¶22. How did you feel when your children began to have ideas of their own? ☐

23. How did you feel when your children reached their teen years? ☐

¶24. Where did you get advice when you had worries about your children? ☐

¶25. Were there any wars while your family was growing up? ☐

26. If so, how did the war affect your family life?   ☐

27. What were your worries about the war?   ☐

¶28. How did your family live during the Depression?   ☐

29. What kinds of problems were there and how did you deal with them during the Depression?   ☐

¶30. When did each of your children leave home?   ☐

31. How did you feel when each child left?   ☐

¶32. Looking back, what do you think are the best ways of raising children?   ☐

33. What advice would you give to people raising children today?   ☐

34. What are the major differences between the times when you were raising your family and raising a family now?   ☐

(Remember, you want to tell things as they were but not if it will hurt someone.)

Chapter 7

Earning
a Living

¶1. What has been your principal job, career,
   or way of earning your living? ☐

   2. How many jobs did you have before your
   main job? ☐

Answer questions 3a through 3j
for each job you had.

(Remember, answer questions 3a through 3j for each job you had)

¶3a. Describe the type of job you had.   ☐

  3b. What were the working conditions?   ☐

  3c. How did you get the job?   ☐

  3d. How much were you paid?   ☐

  3e. Were you able to live on that pay?   ☐

  3f. How long did you work at that job?   ☐

  3g. What did you think of that job?   ☐

  3h. Why did you stop working at that job?   ☐

  3i. How did you feel when you stopped working at that job?   ☐

  3j. What was your next job?   ☐

¶4. What was the reason you entered your main job field?   ☐

5. What made you decide to remain with that job field to make it your lifetime work?   ☐

6. How has your work changed over the years?   ☐

7. How have your co-workers changed over the years?   ☐

8. Have you noticed changes in skills and attitudes in your co-workers over the years? If so, in what ways?   ☐

9. How have working conditions changed over the years of your working career?   ☐

10. Describe a typical working day at your job.   ☐

¶11. What low points did you reach during your working career?   ☐

12. What caused these low points?   ☐

13. How did you overcome those low points?   ☐

¶14. What high points did you reach during your working career?   ☐

15. What do you consider the main accomplishment of your working years?   ☐

¶16. What do you consider the most valuable things you've learned from your years of working?   ☐

¶17. Judging from your own experience, what would you advise young people today who are looking for work?   ☐

18. What would you tell young people to look for in a job?   ☐

19. What encouragement would you give young people who are trying to find a job or decide upon a career?   ☐

¶20. Looking back, what do you think is most important for people to remember about working?   ☐

Chapter 8

Retirement

¶1. When did you first think about retirement? ☐

2. What was your attitude toward retirement when you were young? ☐

3. When you were a young adult, at what age did people retire? ☐

4. When you were a young adult, how and where did retired people live? ☐

5. When you were a young adult, what did retired people do? ☐

¶6. When did you seriously start thinking about and planning for your retirement?   ☐

7. How have general attitudes toward retirement changed in our country during your adult years?   ☐

8. How have general retirement circumstances changed during your adult years?   ☐

¶9. When did you retire?   ☐

10. Did you have some specific retirement goals or dreams?   ☐

11. Have you been able to work toward or accomplish any of those goals or dreams?   ☐

¶12. How did you feel when you retired?   ☐

13. What emotional adjustments did you face when you retired?   ☐

14. How did you deal with each of those adjustments?   ☐

15. Has anything about retirement been especially difficult for you? If so, describe it and what you've done about it.   ☐

¶16. Is retirement anything like you thought it would be? ☐

¶17. Can you make ends meet on your retirement income? ☐

18. How have you been able to adjust your budget with prices continually rising? ☐

19. Do Social Security or your pension benefits prevent you from working to earn extra income? ☐

¶20. Do you belong to any active groups that are trying to gain rights and considerations for retired people? ☐

21. If so, what groups and how do they go about gaining their goals? ☐

¶22. Do you belong to any recreation groups or travel clubs? If you do, which ones and what do you do with the group? ☐

¶23. Are you in good health? ☐

24. If so, how do you maintain your good health? ☐

25. If not, what health problems do you have? ☐

26. How do you deal with your health problems? ☐

¶27. What advice would you give to your children and grandchildren regarding health?   ☐

¶28. Looking back, what advice about retirement would you give your grandchildren regarding each of the following topics?

    a. pension benefits   ☐

    b. Social Security   ☐

    c. general finances   ☐

    d. housing   ☐

    e. health insurance   ☐

    f. employment   ☐

    g. transportation   ☐

¶29. What have been the worst things about retirement to you?   ☐

¶30. What have been the best things about retirement to you?   ☐

¶31. What do you look forward to accomplishing in the years ahead?   ☐

Chapter 9

Creativity

Though you may not think of yourself as being creative, every person is outstanding in some way. One of my friends, for example, is extremely talented at listening to people and asking questions. Another has been adept at surviving as a typist in business. Another has made the world's most durable rocking chairs and swings for his grandchildren. My grandmother wouldn't think of herself as an artist but her crocheted afghans, tablecloths, and doilies are priceless to the family. So think about your special abilities and talents and then write about them as you see them.

¶1. What do you think has been your most important accomplishment?   ☐

2. Why did that turn out to be your most important accomplishment so far?   ☐

3. How did it come about that you accomplished it?   ☐

4. How long did it take you to accomplish it?   ☐

¶5. What do you consider to be your outstanding talent, ability, craft, or skill?   ☐

6. How did you discover your talent or ability, or how did you get involved with that particular craft or skill?   ☐

7. How long did it take you to learn your craft or skill, or how long to perfect your talent or ability?   ☐

¶8. Who were your most important teachers in developing your talent or ability, or learning your craft or skill?   ☐

9. What has been the most exciting or most outstanding result of your talent, ability, craft, or skill?   ☐

¶10. If you have written any stories or poems, include them here. If they're too long for this section, put them in the appendix.   ☐

11. If your work is too large to include here or to put in the appendix, where do you keep it?   ☐

12. Where can your children, grandchildren, or great-grandchildren see your work?   ☐

Chapter 10

Highlights and Special Thoughts

¶1. Looking back now, what do you consider to be the most difficult time or event of your life?   ☐

2. What made it the most difficult time?   ☐

3. How did you deal with that difficult time?   ☐

(Remember to write frankly and in detail. Knowing what you did may help your children, grandchildren, and great-grandchildren to solve their difficulties more effectively.)

¶4. If you had it to do over again, would you make any changes in the way you handled that difficult period?   ☐

¶5. Again looking back, what do you consider to be the best time of your life?   ☐

6. What made it the best time of your life?   ☐

¶7. Who have been your best friends over the years?   ☐

8. How did you become friends with each one?   ☐

9. What do you think are the ingredients of true lasting friendships?   ☐

¶10. Throughout your life, what books have you found to be your favorites? Why?   ☐

¶11. What have been your favorite stories, and why?   ☐

¶12. What have been your overall favorite plays, movies, or television programs? Why were these your favorites?   ☐

¶13. What sayings, thoughts, or proverbs have you used that have helped you throughout your life?   ☐

14. Where did you learn those thoughts, sayings, or proverbs?   ☐

¶15. What do you think has been your overall guide or formula for living?   ☐

¶16. Looking back, who or what do you think has been most influential or inspirational in forming your way of living?   ☐

¶17. What do you think is the most important guideline, philosophy, or rule a young person today should live by?   ☐

18. Why do you think so?   ☐

Appendixes

Appendix 1

Photographs of Family Importance

You may wish to include some photographs. If you don't want to part with the originals, a photography store or studio can make copies of the pictures for you, even if you no longer have the negatives. Be sure to identify the people or places in the photographs and to put the dates the pictures were taken, if you can remember. Mount the pictures on sheets of paper the same size as those you have been writing on. Or you may prefer to put them in a pocket inside a ring binder—if that is how you "bind" your "book."

Appendix 2

Favorite Heirlooms To Share

What are your favorite recipes, patterns, or directions for making things? What are the instructions for your favorite hobby or craft? Insert them, if you wish, for your family to use.

Appendix 3

Family Tree

Fill out the following family tree charts as completely as you can, then clip out and put at the end of your autobiography. If there are stories about some of the relatives that you think your grandchildren would enjoy, write the stories on pages following the charts.

My Family
(Mother's Side)

Maternal great-grandmother:

_____

Birth date: _____   If deceased, date: _____

Maternal great-grandfather:

_____

Birth date: _____   If deceased, date: _____

Notes about family:

Maternal grandmother:

_____

Birth date: _____   If deceased, date: _____

Maternal grandfather:

_____

Birth date: _____   If deceased, date: _____

Notes about family:

Children	Birth date:	If deceased, date:

Children	Birth date:	If deceased, date:

My Family
(Father's Side)

Paternal great-grandmother:

_____

Birth date: _____   If deceased, date: _____

Paternal great-grandfather:

_____

Birth date: _____   If deceased, date: _____

Notes about family:

Paternal grandmother:

_____

Birth date: _____   If deceased, date: _____

Paternal grandfather:

_____

Birth date: _____   If deceased, date: _____

Notes about family:

Children	Birth date:	If deceased, date:
_____	_____	_____
_____	_____	_____
_____	_____	_____
_____	_____	_____
_____	_____	_____
_____	_____	_____
_____	_____	_____

Children	Birth date:	If deceased, date:
_____	_____	_____
_____	_____	_____
_____	_____	_____
_____	_____	_____
_____	_____	_____
_____	_____	_____
_____	_____	_____

Immediate Family

Mother:

_____

Birth date: If deceased, date:

_____   _____

Father:

_____

Birth date: If deceased, date:

_____   _____

Notes about family:

Spouse:

_____

Birth date: If deceased, date:

_____   _____

Children	Birth date:	If deceased, date:
_____	_____	_____
_____	_____	_____
_____	_____	_____
_____	_____	_____
_____	_____	_____
_____	_____	_____
_____	_____	_____
_____	_____	_____
_____	_____	_____
_____	_____	_____

Date of marriage: _____

Place of marriage: _____

Immediate Family
(Continued)

Children

Name:

_____

Birth date: If deceased, date:

_____

Spouse:

_____

Birth date: If deceased, date:

_____

Date of Marriage: Place of Marriage:

_____

Name:

_____

Birth date: If deceased, date:

_____

Spouse:

_____

Birth date: If deceased, date:

_____

Date of Marriage: Place of Marriage:

_____

Grandchildren	Birth date:	If deceased, date:

Grandchildren	Birth date:	If deceased, date:

Immediate Family
(Continued)

Children

Name:

_____

Birth date: If deceased, date:

_____   _____

Spouse:

_____

Birth date: If deceased, date:

_____   _____

Date of Marriage: Place of Marriage:

_____   _____

Name:

_____

Birth date: If deceased, date:

_____   _____

Spouse:

_____

Birth date: If deceased, date:

_____   _____

Date of Marriage: Place of Marriage:

_____   _____

Grandchildren	Birth date:	If deceased, date:
_____	_____	_____
_____	_____	_____
_____	_____	_____
_____	_____	_____
_____	_____	_____
_____	_____	_____
_____	_____	_____

Grandchildren	Birth date:	If deceased, date:
_____	_____	_____
_____	_____	_____
_____	_____	_____
_____	_____	_____
_____	_____	_____
_____	_____	_____

My Family

Great-grandchildren	Birth date:	If deceased, date:
_____	_____	_____
_____	_____	_____
_____	_____	_____
_____	_____	_____
_____	_____	_____
_____	_____	_____
_____	_____	_____
_____	_____	_____
_____	_____	_____
_____	_____	_____
_____	_____	_____
_____	_____	_____
_____	_____	_____
_____	_____	_____

Notes about family:

Notes about family:

Appendix 4

How To Bind Your Autobiography

Now put all the pages of your writing in order with the appendix sections in the back.

Congratulations! You have just completed a priceless gift for your family. Without you, your family could never have this record of their heritage to treasure and to pass along to future generations.

You can bind your work into book form in several ways. You may wish merely to punch holes in the sides of the pages and put them in a ring binder—perhaps one with pockets to hold mementos of various kinds.

Should you wish more formal or permanent binding you may use binding services that may be available in your town or some nearby larger city. They are usually listed under "Bookbinders" in the yellow pages of your phone directory. Some copying services have inexpensive methods, or you may wish to locate a regular bookbinder to put a cloth or leatherette cover on your work, making it an heirloom of durability and beauty.